Jehovah, God of Battles, Up to Date

THE GERMAN GOD
A SOLILOQUY BY WILLIAM II ON THE EVE OF PALM SUNDAY, 1918

By

HARVEY M. WATTS, A.M., LITT.D.

Author of "The Wife of Potiphar, with other Poems," "The Faith of Princes," "Pennsylvania," "Lux Erat," "Over There," etc., etc.

PHILADELPHIA
THE JOHN C. WINSTON COMPANY
1919

WRITTEN FEBRUARY–MARCH, AND READ BEFORE THE
PHI BETA KAPPA AT THE UNIVERSITY OF PENNSYLVANIA,
MAY THE FIRST, NINETEEN HUNDRED AND EIGHTEEN

"THE GRAVE OVER THERE"

I KNOW a little mound that waits for me,
   For, though 'tis flower-besprent and flag-en-
      twined,
Yet none who knew the clay have there inclined
And kissed the earth that holds him fair and free,
Knowing his worth, at rest eternally,
And what he means to those of kin and kind,
Who, some day, risking pain of body, mind,
Would grateful kneel there in humility.—
O little grave, o'er there on shot-torn lea
No soil is alien or unconsecrate
Where he, amid the shell-fire, lies at peace!
Whose death has put us in his solemn fee
As comes the dawn of man's supreme estate
When love shall waken and all wars shall cease!

PREFACE

IN THE winter of 1918, at a time when the gloomiest foreboding as to the possible temporary success of Might prevailed, the desire was never overcome to write a pendant to the anticipations of Teutonic frightfulness and the universal application by the German mind of Machiavelli's "force, fraud and guile," as set out in my soliloquy of Cesare Borgia in "The Faith of Princes"—written in December, 1914, and published in 1915—and to prophesy the downfall of Kaiserism through the intervention of America. As events moved, however, the poem when read before the University of Pennsylvania Chapter of the Phi Beta Kappa on May 1st was considered somewhat daring in its open acceptance of the doom of William II as certain and even when printed in July was reviewed more often as a broad presentation of the

arrogant philosophy of Germany's "will to
Power"—to use the German pedant's cant-
ing phrase—through the Hohenzollern as
the spokesman of the people's horrible
ambitions than for its direct pen-picture of
the Imperial leper at the end of his rope.
With William the absconder, the laughing
stock of the whole world, with none so
foolish as to do him reverence, the coda of
the poem now takes on the significance of
a prophecy that has come true. The
exposition of the arch-criminal's plans and
hopes—"he would agree with every word
you have written and would only wonder
how you got his conceits down so pat"
writes a friendly counsellor—in the sec-
tions that lead up to the coda becomes
therefore, it is hoped, a kind of ready refer-
ence, a convenient and almost autobio-
graphical and self-revelatory summary of the
Evil Thing that the Teutonic mind evoked
to the counter-point of the Wagnerian sword
motif and the Nibelungen philosophy. An

Evil Thing which is already a dimming
memory of an almost unimaginable and
hideous nightmare of stark unrealities, but
which, in February–March, 1918, what with
the Hohenzollern bombast still clogging the
cables and the Siegfried, Brunnhilde, Alber-
ich and Wotan battle lines in France still
impregnable, was a very appalling reality
indeed.

H. M. W.

January 1, 1919.

JEHOVAH, GOD OF BATTLES, UP TO DATE

THE GERMAN GOD

Victory!

Allegro Energico.

Soliloquy by William II on the eve of Palm Sunday, 1918.

Scene—The Cabinet de Travail in the Palace at Potsdam.

The Kaiser is looking out at the window over the park which darkens under the spring twilight. By his side, on a small table, lies an antique sword, Roman, with straight T-shaped handle, and a large Bible with many slips of crimson ribbon inserted in its pages to indicate certain books and texts upon which he has requested memoranda from the Imperial Chaplains and Pastors in order to pick out the text for the victory sermon.

Through the closed doors of the Cabinet come, at times, the faint tones of a piano on which some attaches of the Palace are playing. Fragments from the Nibelungen music drama are heard and particularly the "Song of the Sword" from Siegfried. As the Kaiser's ear catches the Sword Motif he takes his hand from the Bible which he was about to open, beats time on the window pane with his finger and exclaims:

JAH, "Nothung, Nothung, neidliches
  Schwert," indeed!
  Jah, "Todt lagst du in Trummern
dort," too long!
But now this blade, the German sword's alive,
Its motif sounds through all the quickened
  earth,.
Its long-time forging true was not in vain.
The Master never wrote a better line;
Nor more prophetic, though most ears were
  dull
And eyes were blind to what it signified.

From Rheingold to the final score the call
Thrills every soul who knows his race and
 name;
The German folk, whose ways were e'er of
 peace,
Yet, trained by me, know how to go to war;
Sons of the sword, Lords of the flashing
 blade,
"Die Falschen" shattered as by Siegfried's
 might,
As France, wild for revenge, lured by the
 lies,
The lies of Albion, is spent at last,
Snared and betrayed by friends as false as
 weak,
Whose punishment, delayed, is certain, sure,
As "hands across the sea" stretch emptily,
The gestures, like the words, full impotent!
Since time fights with and for us to the last
Our dice are loaded with the weight of men,
Our heavier battalions, winners all,
Whose triumph, all the world must now
 confess.

Nor wrought the folk,nor swung they sword,
    in vain;
And so in forge, on farm and battlefront
We have secured and kept our heritage.
Facing the rising sun, we seek our place
And shall not be denied our lot therein;
Since, lo, we celebrate deeds uncompared,
Success beyond all seeming chance and range
Of human prowess, irresistible;
More than we hoped for was predestinate,
As if ripe fruit, or rotten, fell by winds
Sent by our God who smiles upon our cause,
The end made to our hands and by them too.
While we prepare te deums for our hosts,
Our enemies repeat trisagions,
Their kyries our triumph-lieds in fact,
The Dies irae of a world in flames.
But not the "saeclum in favilla" yet;
Since I, protector, not the wrathful judge,
Will save the remnant through our glorious
    peace;
Our peace, not theirs, for so the world is
    bound—

And bound, must look to us to heal its
    wounds,
Must seek the balm of our own Gilead,
That, as of old, awaits my royal touch.
And whom I heal, and whom I shall pass by,
Is all as I elect and God decrees.
But, as I stand the victor, all is plain;
My task is but begun; like husbandman,
With cunning hands upon the worn-out stock
Of ancient cultures, opposites, I'll graft
Our own and let the world bear German fruit,
What'er its origins or race intent.
They well may bend in bough as twig's
    inclined,
And I'll reset as well as find the twig
And fix the inclination at my will.
If they hold back I'll crush the brood of hate
With no more twinges than the gardener
    knows,
Who, booted, stalks along the sanded path,
And treads the myriad ants which idly
    swarm,
A realm in petto, ground beneath his heel!

And so with me the larger purposes,
My own and God's, control. Those who
    oppose
Bring their own ruin as in Belgium
Whose incapacity in time of stress,
Self-violation of the neutral oath,
Deprived it of its separate estate;
And dark Armenia whose hidden plots,
Born of old schisms, ancient heresies,
Fanatic stubborness, have doomed it quite;
And Serbia strutting, when it should have
    crept
Before us humbly, tripped and fell full prone.
The stiff-necked ever thus invite their fate,
And stumbling bring the world about their
    ears.

I WILLED this not, nor planned a world
    at war,
    But those of Islam, men who walk with
    God,
If not in our own way at least in theirs—
How well they walk is lesson to us all—

With vision, say 'tis "Kismet!"   And, of
    truth,
Since God reveals His hand in history,
Gracious to those who know His mind and
    way,
As says the Koran, there is fixed a term
To every Nation and the issue's joined.
When it is passed, no respite, all is o'er;
Chance knocks upon the Door of Life but
    once!
Light hearts, light hands, nor hear the knock
    nor ope,
The feeble beat upon the bolts in vain.
So pass my enemies whose term is up
As I seize all as ready legatee.
Prepared! all things escheat as if by rote.
Unreadiness is its own punishment
As they well know who cry in pain "too late,"
Finding us masters where they idly ruled.
I waste no time o'er their deep miseries;
For weaklings jeopardize all sovereignty;
The chain sums up the weakest link in
    strength.

And laggard nations, which are out of pace,
Shall never clog nor stop our chariot wheels,
Nor shall they halt the progress of the
    world.
Their fell disease calls loudly for the knife,
Lest it contaminate the healthy flesh,
And, like contagion, spread beyond control.
Cruel in deed, am I, but kind in fact,
And know the stroke that cleaves and like-
    wise cleans,
Which, multiplied in war's enmillioned
    might,
Saves by its very menace. For, disguised,
War is the benison for us, for all,
The double blessing to a nation torn;
New valors blossom in the humblest heart,
New virtues spring where once was selfish-
    ness,
And all the folk at one in sacred cause,
Sloughing their sins as if confessed of God,
Are shrived as though before the judgment
    seat.
For lo, while Europe, slothful, lay asleep,

I saw the fiery dragon in the sky,
More frightful than a Fafner; saw, in sooth,
The Yellow Peril, and opposed my might,
Mailed as to fist, and armed from top to toe,
And faced the menace but to see it fade
Before our threat of might and majesty.
Woe, woe to them who stand athwart my
      path.
The Goth is my exemplar to the end,
In Attila I see myself forecast,
Flagella peccatorum, as our Lord.
For I am Jahveh's sword and doubled-edged.
An instrument devoted in his hands;
A scourge of God in fact as well as fame,
Who sums the Hun in all his ruthlessness,
But, like the fire, a cauter and a cure!

SO I have fought the fight and kept the
      faith
      E'en as my allies, quick of ear and
      hand,
Who keep with me the sacred word and strive
Under the banner of the Caliphate.

Pawns in my play who move as I direct.
This is the law of Nations and of right,
The "must" and "ought" of Kant's impera-
     tive,
The category of the ruling mind,
That keeps the conscience and the State as
     one.
This is the inspiration of success,
The cause and conduct of a war most just.
Nations no less than Nature must obey
The universal rule that seeks the fit
And arms them with the right divine to live,
Surviving while their enemies are crushed.
Darwin is ours! his law we have applied
As law of action, superseding cults,
Since war selects unerringly its own.
While some are raised to honor, victis vae!
Treitschke foresaw, foretold, forewarned
     them all
In open prophecy of that great day,
When force and frightfulness the direful
     means,
Direful for those who sat with folded hands,

Would bring the sure result in certain time
As we prepared the nation to a man.
And gave the countersign of hope to all;
Strike without mercy, slay without a trace!
Our knights whose cloak is white if cross be
      black—
The omen is propitious to our cause—
For ever set their seal upon our way;
The olden way that suits our cause today.
And stand the model of our conquering
      hosts.
Who have, in newer Tannenberg, redeemed
Their marshes, reddened with the martyr
      blood
Of those who set our feet upon the path
Of empire through the sure Teutonic soul,
Strengthening the stroke of surer Teuton
      sword,
Time's long-delayed requital at our hands;
Lex talionis, law of tooth and claw,
As we revenge ourselves for all the past,
None left with eyes but those that weep
      their fate!

WAGNER was right, the sword is
over all.
And would a greater might arise to
set
A newer scoring for this flashing steel
Our own Excalibur, a sacred sign!
Our "in hoc signo vinces," by the sword,
And not the cross as Constantine averred,
Who, wearied, saw, on high in Rhenish
lands,
His haloed labarum in blazing sky;
In terror of the omen, full distraught,
Grasped at the shadow and misread the sign.
For, hold the blade with handle upright, so,
The chorus does it very well in "Faust,"
And e'er the blood-wet weapon turns a
cross.
But still for that it is the blade that wins,
And *won* for Constantine as all men know.
So we reverse the omen to our gain.
In signo hoc—The sword our only sign!
Who did not grasp this fact but only knew
The little arc of their own destiny,

Nor saw the greater circle which I scanned,
Have brought this ruin on themselves, the
    fools!
They read the story but to miss the point,
We make the past convenient stepping stones,
Or fingerposts that point the only way,
Or charted seas with all shoals indicate.
And I in Russia have applied the hint
And made their present debtor to our past.
As Friedrich knew that Poland could not
    live
Save as a vassal of a greater line,
Since all things whirl inexorably by law,
Each center with attendant satellites,
Quiring in harmony and lasting peace,
As once proud Rome, the golden hub, con-
    trolled
All destinies.   Gained not by single stroke,
As when Caligula, an ass in boots,
Wished that his enemies had but one neck,
But surely, each in turn, till all were won.
"Divide and conquer," 'twas the ancient
    aim,

Which we apply in quintessential force,
As fortune shows the way and eke the means.
E'en as the Caesars glorified the rule,
Inheritors of all their greater lore,
Roman in all but name, we take our own.
And take it first; by that the game is won.
Enslaved by me the conquered do our tasks.
I leave to them their self-determined way
So long as they promote the end desired;
The end that justifies our every deed.
Nor quarrel I o'er means that get results;
Since war is war, why count the units lost?
The mass is all that matters in the main,
Who counts the eggs that made the omelet?
For omnia prona victoribus was writ
Of England conquered and full bound in
        chains.
Victors the world will grovel at your feet
Where conquered you accept their jibes and
        gyves.
"Auferre, trucidare, rapere,"
Says Tacitus of Britain's ancient woes.
"Yes, rape and rapine," so his venom runs,

"Misnamed as Empire overcame the world."
With appetite beyond the chance to glut,
Since "Quos non Oriens, non Occidens
Et satiaverit," they quote at me.
"Nor East nor West could satisfy their
      greed.
With equal avid wish, abundance, want
The rich, the poor they coveted and seized."
And yet, and yet, their bounds, periphery,
The urbs et orbis, circle of the lands,
Spite of the slanders, words of British hate,
Where'er the conqueror went were blessed
      with peace;
That Pax Romana that redeemed the earth,
As now that peace that comes alone through
      me,
My peace to which I'll dedicate a shrine—
Our Ara Pacis more imperial
Than that Augustus raised with easy fame,
Rome's latest wonder, pigmy though to mine
As Leipzig's monument forecasts in bulk—
And glorify as Pax, Pax Candida,
Shining fore'er as Pax Germanica!

THEY whine o'er this and cry "Atrocities!"
And scream o'er women plotters,
rightly slain,
Of loose-lived soldiers by us crucified,
A warning seen but once not soon forgot,
And quote the Massacre of Innocents.
Well, Herod is traduced through lying text;
The Matthew Gospel stands in this impure.
Then, as of me, they spread the cunning tale,
Maligned the Imperial dignity and power,
Imputed evils that their mind evoked.
But if it were necessity, all's well!
I join the tetrarch, nor condemn the act
When it is done for purposes of State;
Women and children first, lest they should
prove
Impedimenta that might block our way,
Since infants make a ready blind for men
And tottering peasants screen an ambuscade.
So let them prattle of our blood and iron;
And I will answer with the roar of guns.
My Empire is the cannon's farthest range,

Its limits marked alone by force of arms,
Where flies the flag o'er sea, where tread my
      troops!
This is my challenge flung both far and wide.
No bounds of Hercules in narrowed strait
Confine us to the seas as known of old;
The Baltic and the Middle Seas our own,
The ocean turned into a German lake.
This is "Der Tag" we toasted to the skies,
And this expansion is but Nature's law,
And its accomplishment a holy cause,
Our Jehad, dear to me and all my line,
Since our brave banner bears the one device,
As supermen the supramundum cry;
The Fatherland o'er all, o'er all the world.

VICTOR abroad, at home my will is
      law
     In court and temple, fane and syna-
      gogue,
Semite and anti-Semite do my will,
And all the Christian faiths hang on my
      word.

No bleak Canossa lies before my path,
Matilda's fame is "writ in water;" bah!
The Vatican's decrees sing small indeed,
They talk of "peace," "impartiality";
I laugh aloud, indeed, both first and last,
And who would not who stands behind the
    scenes
And moves them all; mere marionettes that
    dance
As puppet rulers as I pull the strings.
Their non-cathedra murmurings are vain,
Mere tinkling brass, solemn but empty
    sound.
My sanction supersedes their canon law,
Their "imprimatur" is my manual,
The text is theirs, the inspiration mine.
They know a Fontainebleau awaits them all,
So they dissemble, and, with feeble show
Of power, "thunder in the indices,"
Unheard beyond the Tiber's muddy banks,
And there unknown save in Trastevere
Within the Pope's own court of Damasus.
Our Cardinals, 'tis true, have all the port

And ancient pomp of princes of the realm.
He of Cologne is Bourbon to the hat,
As arrogant as Hildebrand himself,
But Hildebrand in exile knew the day
Of disillusion and of shattered hopes,
The punishment for pride that rode to fall.
The Countess failed him at the last, his
    threats
Re-echoed idly in St. Angelo;
Things not set out in Papal histories.
Today they'd play the same old, worn-out
    tricks
With Munich as their latest stalking horse,
Where, lo, the Civil hides the Prelate's robe.
But I will thwart them at the proper time;
They know not Luther, Reuchlin is forgot,
Erasmus as if not, but we shall see.
A newer Kultur-kampf may ope their eyes,
The Sistine know the calibre of guns,
And dogma yield to lay majorities
When backed by bombs and zeppelins in
    flight
And all to force, and so the circle's run.

Yet they extend my person and my power
Since all must bow before me and obey.
Just as the Jews, though ingrates, are of use;
In race apart they know no Nation's heart,
Exiled, "dispersed" from far Judean soil,
They, like Antaeus out of touch with earth,
Have lost their fighting spirit once their wont
And find their "Promised Land" in lanes of
      trade,
The "milk and honey" in the interest rate.
Unstable as a woman's whims they cower,
But garner where our steel has reaped the
      grain.
Their bankers cried that they "would have
      no war."
Poof, poof, like down before the gale their
      weight
When war broke out and boundaries dis-
      appeared,
And credit, like the laws, or stood or fell
As arms determined and the battle's gage.
I'll teach them what the Ghetto really
      means,

I'll have the synagogues reform their ways,
And quote the prophets to sustain my throne.
And new phylacteries shall spell my wish,
Instead of mumbo-jumbo for a text
Mere amulets of Bedouins at the best.
If they plot anarchy as is the wont
Of kith and kin in Russia, vermin all,
They'll face a Pale from Posen to the sea
And know the clink of something else than
    gold.

B UT I full know their cultus helps my
    cause,
    For e'en the Koran is a mine of
    wealth,
Its Suras filled with pregnant rules of life,
Of racial law, domestic wisdom too,
Since all the East is wise in its own way.
And we may profit while we hold our own
Compelling tribute to the State's one aim,
Its strength in numbers knowing but our will.
But this is vain if numbers melt away
Before the stress of war without recoup

And men and women turn to epicenes—
Forgetting "Male and female made He
     them"
Like to the birds in air, the beasts in field
Nor spoiled by manners of the close or cage—
As pundits quarrel over customs, means,
And crown virginity with claustral phrase,
And empty cradles menace e'en the throne.
Man-strength is but the babe-in-arms of age.
Yet we sit idle while the sands run out
And think of marriage as a chance caprice,
One man, one mate, as if the law of God.
Not so the record nor the unbroken rule,
As my professors, quick on ancient ways,
Eager to serve me with safe precedents
Of customs certified by sure results
And fitted to our modern idiom,
Rooted in Ayran race and origin,
Have proved in brochures irrefutable!
The Talmud, in the face of facts, allows
The long familiar habit of the folk,
Yet sets no seal, no more than Islam does,
Of prim approval on the equal bond

Of twain as one, since need must e'er decide
The moral obligations of the State.
And I decide what custom must approve;
The State's summed up in me and fixed in
      mine!
And in this crisis, lo, our course is clear,
One duty falls with equal force on all.
As war upsets the olden rule of life,
The law, command divine, "Increase and
      multiply";
The cornerstone by God, ordained of old,
Should be for us a potent lease of power.
Mahomet proved the seer in this, nor stood
Upon lax preachments; yet, we, weak, recoil,
E'en though the Mormon State has proved
      anew
That chastity is but the soul's intent.
The home is oft the harem, thin disguised,
And childless, loveless, too, a hollow sham,
So out upon this cheap hypocrisy
And let us take the lesson to our hearts,
Find newer virtue in new sacrifice.
Let women ne'er forget their "rule of three,"

Church, chores and children, sole and only
    aim,
And make the family, as of old, the fount
And firm foundation of a lasting State.
Nor hazard future years by false ideas.
The people at their best, our brawn and
    brain,
Are but the shadow of my competence.
And I will shape them to our signal ends.
Yea, "regis voluntas suprema lex,"
My will *is* law in forum and in field!

I STAND upon the pinnacle of fame,
    A new Assyria rises into view.
    Austria, my vassal, at my beck and call,
With kings and princes as my satrapies,
For Alexander, Caesar, Charlemagne,
Ne'er knew such triumphs as are ours by
    arms.
For lo, as from a lofty mountain height
The Kingdoms of the world laid out in plan,
Reticulate as if from 'plane in flight,
Are spread as feast before my searching eyes,

Which catch a glory of the Greater East
Reflecting glory of the Greater West.
Theodoric who flung his mighty dare
O'er the Isonzo set for me the pace;
And with Napoleon in Egyptian sands
I've looked to Gaza and to Lebanon,
"Partant Pour Syrie" as my lullaby,
And sensed the Orient in golden dreams,
My fancy visioning its strange delights
As Haroun trod the streets in chance dis-
    guise,
And intrigue, in the cloak of sheer Romance,
Gave Narrative compelling mystery.—
So, musing o'er the magic of its lands,
Wondrous their past and possibilities,
Whose plains have ever held my deep desires,
Whose hills my ardent hopes, where old and
    new
Meet on the shining way that leads at last
Past Bagdad to the seas that wash the Ind
Under the yellow moon of Schahriar,
Beneath the rose tree where old Omar sleeps,
And through the fastnesses of Afghan gorge,

With Delitsch I have lived the lives of old,
Restored in splendor Asshurbanipal,
Symbol of all my plans of empiry,
Spawned in the East, perfected in the West.
A second Constantine, I, on the Rhine,
Which, safely German, laves its banks in
      peace,
No longer subject to Ovidian sneers,
The "Rhenus squalidus" 'midst "broken
      reeds,"
Shall, lo, evoke the West that is our East
And East that's West as our own leaven
      works.
Russia my footstool, washpot, too, in fact,
The Euxine held by us in simple fee,
The Golden Horn, a bauble in our hands,
The Drang nach Osten realized at last;
Where we may bask and stretch ourselves
      at ease,
Yes, in the sun at his meridian height.
For I have trod the Holy Land and gazed
In silence on grey-walled Gethsemane,
And, from on high, on sloping Olivet,

Saw mine own tower o'er Jerusalem,
Triumphant rising in the Muristan;
Above all domes and minarets supreme,
Supreme o'er David's tower and battle-
      ments;
A prophecy of my intent and will.
And had they read it better for them all.
For more was broken down than olden walls
And parapets of Solymein the Great,
When, through the breach that looks toward
      Joppa, I,
Acclaimed by all, came in a Paladin,
In shining panoply in knightly guise,
A second Barbarossa, aye, in state,
And shared the privileges oft denied
The great in dim and inner secret shrines.
Damascus too paid tribute to my aim;
Like Saul I found there my apostolate.
With eager ardor as of convert's zeal,
In prayer before the tomb of Saladin,
In firm resolve to follow where he lead,
I pressed the lesson of unscabbared might;
"Protector of the Faithful" for all time.

With my Megiddo not a threshing floor,
Scant in extent if meeting-place of kings,
Ensanguined by the blood of centuries,
But world-wide in its swelling amplitude!
Had I but gone to Mecca, Ah, in truth,
Arabia at my feet, the desert bound
In fealty of faith to my own whims,
Would follow, camel-wise, where'er I led.
I'll have a fetva yet, for what are creeds
To those who tread the higher ways of life—
And King and Kaiser, I'll be Caliph too;
Lord of all Asia and the whirling globe.

A NEWER Petrus, I; I, too, have seen
The vision of the heavenly sheet let
down
And know the meaning of the clear com-
mand
"Consider nothing common or unclean!"
We Germans know our destiny, our fate,
Our learning is for all a tonic draft
Of living waters from the sacred rock,
A panacea seen by Malachi,

That Sun of Righteousness whose radiant
    beams
Light up the earth with glory all its own.
Through me the synthesis of all belief,
The universal solvent, Alcahest,
Philosophy with all its dross expurged,
Becomes the touchstone of my people's weal.
For gods are made in man's own image, aye,
And badly made at that in foolishness
As all the deities invent, attest.
Chemosh and Marduk, Moloch all are one
Squabbling like vultures o'er the carrion
    fields
Of war, and eager for the praise of men;
The praise of men who cry them, "Victors
    all!"
These be the gods of old, e'en Israel's—
Jahveh is Judah 'tween the cherubim,
While "Allah" is but Arab written large.
The desert spawns its prophets as the sand
Yields up the incense-bearing shrubbery.
The elders walk with God, the young cry out
Their burning visions to the passers-by;

The very "res angustae" give them point.
When gaunt of body, lo, the soul expands,
And, starved at home, they spread their
    truths abroad,
For logothetes were early in the field
In Babylon as at Byzantium.
But I would strike the balance with them all.
Combine the logos with the blade that rules.
But for the sword, Mohammed might have
    mused
Upon the Meccan housetops all in vain,
Hailed as a babbler, dreamer of vain dreams,
And jeered and hooted in the market place.
But, lo, when from Medina swept his horde,
Fire in their eye and fury in their heart,
Who neither asked, nor quarter gave, in
    sooth,
The Empire rose again in the Eastern lands,
And Allah and his prophet claimed their
    due.
And like Jehovah, or the earlier line
Of village deities, the parish bonds
Were burst asunder by the feat of arms,

And swift dominion came with sword and
    book
And book proved by the sword became the
    law.
As our Kultur is now before the world.
For, in the melting-pot, faiths equalize;
And so with Allah mine, our Lord still
    shrined,
Yet I am not unmindful of our own,
The ancient runes of wood-folk, hero-bred,
Who know the fetish and its magic power;
The Bismarck "turms" upon the ancient
    heights,
Druidic altars of the empire's birth,
Like Baal-fires kindled as a warning sign;
Or, as our Mars, the giant Hindenburg,
Colossal idol of the people's hopes,
Studded with golden nails, a new taboo
Our procul, procul, O, profani, Ah,
The Ur-mind harking to its olden call.
An avatar of ancient fearlessness,
An Ariovistus in the flesh once more.
But, lo, a chief whom fortune never fails—

The jade does ever favor those who seize
Her by the scruff, deaf to all niceties—
Thus we improve the breed and sturdy stock,
React to all the heart-pull of the race.
And, as the Valkyrs sweep the darkening sky,
With neigh of horse and scurry of the hoofs
And flash of fire mid thunder in the vault,
Our Wotan, Thor and Loki rise in sight
Our Northern forbears, yes, our three in one,
Their contradictions all resolved by me,
The Norns the servants of my destiny.
Myself the arbiter of fate and faith
Et deum inveniam aut faciam,
I'll find a god or make one to my taste—
Since by my right on earth, vice regent, I,
In essence Godlike in my Majesty
Summus episcopus, I thus declare
This thing amalgamate from Holy Writ,
Disjecta membra of the old beliefs,
Welded be me, as Siegmund's broken shards
Into the tempered blade that nought with-
    stood,
The Norseland sagas, Islam's litanies,

The Vedic Hymns and Iran's mystic rites,
Lore of the East and wisdom of the West,
Jehovah, God of Battles, up to date,
Improved by me in world-compelling cult,
Once tribal now shall dominate the earth:—
Judea's hilltop Lord, the German God,
Der alte Gott der Deutschen und der Welt,
But ruling not alone, aye, not alone!

THE PEACE OF JOSHUA

Allegro Trionfale.

The Kaiser turns abruptly, picks up the Bible and begins to finger the different marked places, his eye lighting up as he notes the familiar and favorite texts and, carefully readjusting certain of the markers, he continues his musing:

THEY ask me to select the victory text.
    Aye, they do well—It must be done with care,
With full regard to our dynastic claims

And what this people mean before the world.
I will not have a war of petty creeds
Splitting thin hairs of doctrine in my cause.
In this great moment of the Empire's life,
One thought, one mind, one heart, one hope
      is ours,
The pulpit may embellish, give its gloss,
And suit the language to its auditors,
Simple or high and rich or poor or great,
Small is the difference so they follow me;
As ships lie moored at anchorage and veer
And float this way and that as shifts the tide,
But ever steadfast to the hidden chains
That keep them in the channel and the
      course,
So I would hold all anchored to my will
And to the word that vindicates our cause.
To fix the mob-mind is a care of State.
And these the shepherds of the flock should
      learn
How best to drive and what the path shall be.
I'll have the rectors work the problem out
And let the pastors echo my ideas,

With each professor prophesying too.
The text, from Old or New, it matters not,
Save that the message ring out loud and
    clear
With due respect to what the sword has won
These are the compass points of my concern,
The North and South of all my policy.
No Caesar, pontifex as well as dux,
E'er saw a world so helpless at his feet.
My apotheosis at last is nigh;
The auguries must be manipulate,
The signs uphold me in my deep designs.
I'll brook no play of empty phrase to prove
Some fond perversion of plans foreordained.
No; nothing left to chance lest feeble wits,
Whose hearts are not much softer than their
    heads,
Should seek with muddled vision to confuse
The growing testament that vindicates
Our every deed—The Law, the Prophets, too,
The Gospel and Epistles, word for word,
Whose myriad texts like clouds of witnesses
Yield richest savor, incense for our cause

Interpreted by rubrics all mine own.
So those who cry of "ploughshares, pruning
      hooks,"
Like children playing on the cliff edge stand
In slippery places menaced by my wrath.
For I will none of this; hew to the line,
Stand by your guns, exult and magnify!

E'EN Jesus, who is Joshua new spelled—
    A Joshua too much compassionate
    Whose views are not in full accord
      with mine,
Yet hath He said, "To Caesar render all
Of tribute that is his and eke to God
The measure that is His in equal part."
So thus he recognized the state supreme—
They would misquote. And yet He counsels
      war—
Bernhardi notes it in his argument—
Cries out, "I come not here to send you
      peace,
But lo, a sword, as is my father's wish."
He knew his mission as do I know mine.

But as the clangors of the bells succeed
The diapason of the battlefields,
I fain would quote the elder texts that
     breathe
The throb and threat of men in bloody
     shock;
Texts filled with wrath divine that seeks
     no peace:—
"Their youth shall die, no remnant shall be
     left,
The men of Anathoth shall know our God,
The Lord of Hosts, and die there by His
     sword."
So Jeremiah strikes the tonic key,
And with him is Ezekiel, whose words
Roll out and on as distant sound of drums,
Bold hymns of conquest and of hearty hate.
They sing the old song of the sword, not
     new,
As, lo, it slaked its thirst in thousands slain
As God reached down among Judean hills,
And cities fell, their smoke a cloud by day
And fiery pillar in the purple night.

Why palter we, or falter, when we read
The adjuration all so plainly writ:
Exult with these of old who slew and sang,
And sang just as they slew, as we do now.
But no one text can satisfy today.
I would a chorus sang in sweeping tones,
The words of Deborah in ecstacy;
Or with the timbrel followed Miriam's song,
For she rejoiced in Pharaoh's hosts o'er-
    whelmed
And knew her God was lord of those who
    fight.
Yea, shout aloud so that the world may
    hear:—
"For Saul has slain his thousands," Oh,
    rejoice,
"And David multiplied the blow by tens."
Paltry these numbers as we count our dead,
A thousand thousand and still incomplete,
Laid on the altar of the Fatherland,
A willing offer from us all to bind
With blood my august rule and sacred
    throne!

THEY send Ecclesiastes for a text;
    For says the Preacher well, There's
       time to love,
And time to hate, yes hate, and time to war,
And then, in sooth, he holds a time of grace.
The kind of grace is matter for our will.
But Samuel, Kings and both the Chronicles
Bear witness that our conquest is of right.
We are the besom of the living God,
The chosen to secure His righteous rule.
Fools, fools, who pass by Judges, Genesis,
Nor know the lessons taught by Exodus.
Each verse and chapter forms the Book of
      Fate;
A light unto my path, a lamp, indeed,
To mine own feet that took the open road.
The road that ends in victory supreme!
King David is our hope for every act,
Reprisals have God's full authority:
"Reward them as they serve thee," thus
      one Psalm,
"And happy they who take the little ones
And dash their heads against the very stones."

Nor do the others fail me in support,
My favorite, the Ninety-third, rings true,
Drysander uses it with marked effect.
And when I hear it quoted in the Dom,
Or sung as Psalter, to myself I cry
'Tis I; they sing of me, I'm Majesty,
The words but changed, the phrases are of
 me,
"The Lord is clothed with Majesty and
 strength,
His throne is, yea, of old, and is not moved,
The Testimonies of his words are sure,
And, mightier than the sea in all its rage,
The voice of many nations and the storm,
Is Majesty upon its awful throne."
My throne IS awful as I sit the judge
Upon these people who provoke my wrath.
And then the Twenty-fourth is balm indeed,
Balm and the wind that stirs the very
 soul.
Strange that the Pastoral, the Twenty-third,
That "babbles of green fields" and quiet
 pools,

Of shepherds gently guarding tender sheep,
Should preface such a vision of my might.
For what is this?   "Lift up your heads, ye
      gates,
Be lifted up, ye everlasting doors,
Be lifted that the King"—aye, what a line!—
"The King of Glory may come in in pomp.
Who is the King of Glory?"   How it stirs!
"The Lord of Hosts, of Sabaoth, is King,"
Indeed my king fore'er, and, as I read,
I see myself in cavalcade sweep through
The Brandenburger gate while all cry out
"Our King of Glory is come in!"   Or, more,
In that great dream of dreams, when 'neath
      the Arch,
The Arch of Triumph, with its chains
      removed,
I stride, the Master, "Lift your heads, ye
      gates!
And be ye lifted, everlasting doors,"
The crowd should cry aloud as if compelled
By awe of me, the All-highest, as they see
The princes join in homage as I pass.

AND now the day of Palms, the day of
days,
Is here at last, the day long prophe-
sied.
And as I hear the text, "Hosannah, hail,"
The words ring in my ears as bells of joy,
My accolade from those who know my rights,
"Hosannah, blest the King of Israel,
Who cometh in the name of God Himself."
So John narrates the moving scene of old.
I read it with the inner light and see
Myself in triumph midst the palms, the world,
Remade by me, its ruler, at my feet.
"For, lo, they went before him bearing
palms."
Yes, palmam qui meruit, who more than I?
Ah, that my star combine the Easter burst
Of splendor, and this charnel house of war
Become the open tomb of newer life,
Ne'er sensed by man and known to God alone,
Of newer life and opportunities.—
But to the text, that is my great concern;
Upon its aptness hangs a new success.

The Prophets speak of unrelenting hate
Of those who knew the sword, and, humbled,
    find
Themselves a portion for the foxes, Ah,
"Defile the house and fill the courts with slain,
And multiply them in the streets at will,
The terror of the sword let loose without,
And pestilence within and famine dire,"
"Let Midianites as one be safely slain;
Because the Lord is with those who pursue
The sword of God and Gideon prevails."
What richness in the texts; what range of
    choice!
The lesson must be plain to all, nor hid,
So let all speak and not equivocate.

I'D HAVE them use the Book of Joshua.
   It's full of meat as honeycomb of sweets,
   Telling of Hittite feuds, of Amorites,
Amalekites at bay, then smitten sore;
Leaves nothing out that justifies our wars;
The sack of Ai and haughty Jericho,
Of Gibeon and Hebron in the South;

Of Jericho, whose walls fell prone, nor rose,
Of Gibeon, whose kings fell in their pride
And all the country far and wide laid waste,
Makkedah, Debir, Hazor, in the plains,
The plains of Chinneroth and Gezer, too,
Lachish and Eglon, Libnah by the sword,
The sword of him who stayed the setting sun
And held the wandering moon o'er Ajalon,
The sign and symbol of his victory,
Who fought the foes of God as I have done
And by His favor smote them hip and thigh
From Gaza unto Goshen, nor did rest
Till one-and-thirty kings were in the toils,
Caught in the snare and hanged at fall of night,
Upon the one-and-thirty gibbets hanged,
Then thrown at evening, such the common lot,
In carrion pit, all utterly destroyed
And those who followed stricken to a man,
Nor spared the youth, nor women, babes at
        breast,
Who knew, as God smiled on his handiwork,
In sooth, His peace, the peace of Joshua:
His peace, in truth, the only peace for me.

I'll have this preached within the Dom,
    proclaimed
From all the pulpits throughout all the realm,
That Joshua's peace is our own holy peace,
The peace of Joshua, the son of Nunn,
The peace that's by the sword and of the
    sword,
And for the sword, a lasting peace that holds.
These worthies of the Bible knew their minds
And found their God a not unwilling aid,
As I, as I, the credit where it fits,—
To whom the credit's due, my people know,
So let us to the text and settle all;
I'll put the marker, so, to keep the place,
It lies in Chapter Ten, Verse Forty-two:
"And all the kings and all their utmost lands
Did Joshua take, take in his time, because
Jehovah fought for Israel—"   Enough!
This is the text for me, the victory text,
And let the Pastors cry it everywhere,
The peace of Joshua, the son of Nunn,
Jehovah's peace, won by the sword alone,
A German peace and on our terms at last!

CODA

The Brand of Cain.

Allegro Frenetico-Adagio Solennelle.

*As the Kaiser lays down the Bible a look
of intense satisfaction steals over his face
and his gratification is so great that, as he
gazes into the Park, he hums the lines from
the Lorelei as set to music by Liszt, not the
folk-song version of Silcher, and continues:*

DIE luft ist kuhl—es dunkelt—schnell;
    jah wohl,
    I like the Abbe's setting, Yes, 'tis
    cool,
Und ruhig fliesst der Rhein, der deutsche
    Rhein,
Ah, German still because of our good sword,
Naught else buys peace and keeps it "fest
    und treu;"
Es dunkelt, schnell, I'll have the lights at
    once,

The evening's tranquil as when Goethe wrote
Upon the crystal pane, "O'er all the heights,"
Und uber allen Gipfeln ist Ruh, die Ruh!
"O'er all the heights there shines our
      German peace."
This Easter ecstasy is God's own way.
Und uber allen Gipfeln ist Ruh, die Ruh,
Die Ruh, die Ruh—What, who, who stalks
      within?
What khaki-clothed mummer is this man?
The lights!   The lights!   Es dunkelt,
      schnell, the lights!
A Chaplain with the Stars and Stripes, full
      pale,
His voice, his voice is of the sepulcher.
His words are of the burial liturgy,
Die Luft ist kuhl; I feel a sudden chill.
A text; a text for victory, his words.
What is this mummery, this Bible drip?
A TEXT FOR VICTORY? KNOW THEN
      'TIS WRIT.
THE RACE WILL FAIL INDEED THE
      BOASTFUL SWIFT,

AND PRIDE WILL LOSE THE BATTLE
 FOR THE STRONG.
THY WAR! THY VICTORY! IS GOD
 O'ERTHROWN?
LO HE THAT SITTETH IN THE
 HEAVENS SHALL LAUGH,
IN SHEER DERISION HEAR THEE
 CRY IN VAIN;
SINCE THEY THAT DIG THE PIT
 SHALL FALL THEREIN,
THE FOWLER TRIP HIMSELF IN HIS
 OWN SNARE.
Who speaks in riddles speaks in foolish-
 ness.—
And still he stands! this voice fills all the
 room!
Or is it murmur of the wind in trees?
BLESSED ARE THEY WHO THIRST
 FOR RIGHTEOUSNESS
AND HUNGER FOR IT—THEY SHALL
 ALL BE FILLED.
He would berate me with beatitudes!
And quote the scriptures in contrariness

BLESSED ARE THEY INDEED; THE
    MEEK WITHAL,
THEY SHALL INHERIT—
        Lo, what words are these
In stern monition from his ghastly lips?
BE NOT DECEIVED; GOD IS NOT
    MOCKED,
LO, WHATSOE'ER YE SOW THAT
    SHALL YE REAP.
AND YE THAT DRAW THE SWORD
    AND STRIVE BY IT
SHALL PERISH BY THE SAME, SO
    SAITH THE LORD.
The Hohenzollern way runs counter-wise,
The sword has been our stead for centuries.
VENGEANCE IS MINE, I SHALL
    REQUITE INDEED
AND SAVE YE NEITHER BY THE
    SWORD NOR SPEAR,
YEA, MENE, MENE, TEKEL, UPHAR-
    SIN, HARK!
The words are gibberish as all men know.
The thing deciphered after the event,

A parable for those of kindlich mind,
Kindlich not koniglich as is our own.
THY DAYS ARE NUMBERED AND
    THE END IN SIGHT.
THY KINGDOM IS FOREVER LOST
    TO THEE
Dark sayings, threadbare and without avail,
Repeated oft and so wornout and vain.
AND LO! THE BEAST WHOSE NAME
    WAS BLASPHEMY,
THE HORNÉD BEAST AND CROWNÉD
    WITH THE CROWN,
WHOSE POWER, THOUGH DRAGON-
    GIVEN, WAS NOT FORE'ER.
THY CROWN A RIM OF FIRE UPON
    THY HEAD,
A WRITHING SERPENT-CIRCLET,
    VENOM-FILLED!
Is this a dream, fatigue of war-tired brain,
Or daze from too much pondering o'er the
    texts?
I'll none of it!—Ah, faced, it disappears.
Who reads this riddle must himself be mad,

For Revelation lies 'neath Luther's ban
The canon is in doubt, the text not sure—
WHOSE NAME AND NUMBERS, SIX
    AND SIX AND SIX.
SET OUT THE MONSTER VOID OF
    HEART AND SOUL
THY NAME A HISSING IN THE HALLS
    OF MEN,
A BYE-WORD SPAT WITH HORROR
    FROM THE LIPS.
What boots this anti-Nero haggada,
This Armageddon clatter of the beast,
This anti-Christ, this war of vials and seals.
I'll prove a Daniel in the judgment seat,
And read our primacy in every line,
For prophecy is certain when you know;
And Hebrew numerals arranged at will.
Spell Caesar or the village simpleton.
Still in my ears the voice, the form still
    seen.—
Gott, I have read too long—too long—my
    eyes!
This ringing in my ears—It darkens fast—

What, What; He cries again!
> MEN SHALL DESIRE
> AND SEEK FOR DEATH, SUCH IS
> THEIR WEIGHT OF SHAME,
> AND KNOW THE TORTURES OF THE
> DARK ABYSS,
> THE DARK ABYSS SEALED TO THE
> END OF TIME
> WITH SEVEN SEALS AND SEVEN
> MYSTERIES,
> UPON WHOSE BLOOD-RED SCROLL
> BEHOLD THE MARK,
> THE MARK OF THOSE WHO FALL
> WITH BABYLON,
> WHO FALL WITH BABYLON IN
> LASTING RUIN,
> WHO, IMPIOUS, CLAIMED THE HON-
> ORS DUE TO GOD,
> WITH THE MOST HIGH DISPUTED
> SOVEREIGNTY!
> WEIGHED THOU OF GOD AND
> FOUND AT FAULT IN ALL,

THOU LEAST OF RULERS, LIFE'S
    LONE ISHMAEL.
WHOSE HAND'S AGAINST A WORLD
    ENGULFED IN HATE
AND THEIRS AGAINST HIM.
         Ah, not so, not so!
As God's my judge the sword was forced
    on me!
And I did fight but to defend mine own,
Before all men I swear this solemn truth!
AND PETER SAID UNTO THE LYING
    TONGUE
"BEHOLD THE FEET OF THOSE WHO
    BORE THY MATE
ARE COME IN HASTE WITHOUT."
    SO MEET THY END
FOR YE ARE TOO ABOMINATE OF
    GOD.
AND THEY THAT LOOK FOR THEE
    SHALL SEE THEE NOT,
THOU SHALT INDEED BE BROUGHT
    TO LOWEST HELL,

THE PIT SHALL BE THY FINAL REST-
    ING PLACE,
A CARCASS TRODDEN BY THE FEET
    OF MEN.
AND ALL THE KINGS OF EVIL WHO
    ARE THERE
WILL GREET THEE IN DERISION IN
    ITS DEPTHS.
What is this croaking? Is it of the mind?
Am I alone, or grappling with a shade?
THE WINE-PRESS OF THE WRATH OF
    GOD THY FATE;
THE WINE-PRESS THOU HAST
    FILLED TO RUNNING O'ER.—
TO RUNNING O'ER WITH BLOOD OF
    INNOCENCE,
WHOSE BLOOD CRIES, "VENGE-
    ANCE!" FROM THE TORTURED
    EARTH!
Who flouts the Lord's annointed with these
    words?
Who passes judgment on his regent here?

LO, WHO OFFENDETH THESE OUR
LITTLE ONES,
THE LITTLE ONES WHO PLAY ABOUT
OUR FEET,
BEFORE ALL STANDS AS IF A MILL-
STONE HANGED
ABOUT HIS NECK IN SHAMEFUL
PILLORY.
No, no, mine ears are stopped, mine eyes **are**
closed;
Not mine, not mine the fault! I willed **this**
not.
These wraiths he raises up are not **for**
me;
The Witch of Endor frightened Saul but I,
But I am free of blood guilt, hands
unstained,
Nor fear the fictions of a craven mind.
AND CAIN SLEW ABEL AND WAS
CURSED OF GOD
AND WANDERED FAR AFIELD O'ER
ALL THE EARTH.

The brother's keeper cry once more is
  heard!
And Cain was but a weakling, not so I.
AND CAIN CRIED OUT IN ANGUISH
  OF THE SOUL
"MY PUNISHMENT IS MORE THAN
  I CAN BEAR."
He stands as if St. Michael at the gates
Armed with a flaming sword!   His face!
  his voice!
Bah, it is all a vision!   Help! the
  lights!
Luft! Luft! The lights! The guards! I faint!
  The lights!
UPON THE IMPERIAL BROW THE
  BRAND OF CAIN,
BRANDED FORE'ER BEFORE A
  WORLD OF WOE,
IMPERIAL LEPER BY ALL EXE-
  CRATE.
BARABBAS ON THE CROSS WITH
  FATE DESERVED

AND JUDAS, WHO BETRAYED, KNEW
    FULL REMORSE.
THINK NOT THIS BITTER CUP SHALL
    PASS FROM THEE.
BEHOLD IT IN THY HAND; DRINK
    TO THE DREGS,
THE DREGS OF IGNOMINY, SURE
    DEFEAT!
FOREDOOMED, FOREDAMNED, AND
    ALL THY EVIL LINE,
THY PUNISHMENT—
        No, no—not so—the lights!
Luft—luft—I choke—I faint—es dunkelt,
    Ah—
The brand of Cain—of Cain—of Cain—
    fore'er—
Upon the Imperial brow the brand of Cain—
My punishment is greater—Ah—the dark—
Am ende—luft—the dark—the dark—the
    dark!!
Am ende—Gott—the dark is over all!

Falls heavily to the floor in a swoon.

EPILOGUE

Written November, 1918

Scene.—Early evening; time, November, 1918. A bleak winter landscape in Holland, the distance obscured by the persistent drizzle through which a square Georgian house is seen dimly, with a few windows lit up. In the dripping garden figures move ghost-like on guard about the house and the gateway. Two guardsmen of the Bentinck entourage, in raincoats and caps, with low visors over their foreheads, going off duty, meet before the main entrance and exchange greetings:

First Guard—Well met!   And came the
    German out?
Second Guard—   Not yet,
He sits within and writes and writes and
    writes!
First Guard—What writes he, thinkst thou?

Second Guard—   Lies and lies and lies
And still more lies!
First Guard—   Pursuit congenial I vow
For one whose life was one huge make-
      believe,
Sham and pretense and humbug to the core,
Mere paste-board painted as a sheet of mail!
A mannikin dressed up as Lord of Lands
As hollow as the image of his Gott,
Buffoon and braggart, bully to the last,
Yet once the bladder pricked, complete
      collapse!
Who, craven, with the sceptre lost, but
      whines,
Who once would seize the world now finds
      his sway
By others' favors bound within this park;
Who, seeming glad to eat four meals and
      sleep,
Unmenaced by the whimsies of the mob,
Lo, grasps at servant courtesies as whores
Seek such respect as they may get from dogs;
Grateful indeed for anything that fawns

Since it recalls an honester estate.—
So this imperial prostitute gains hope,
Since e'en cajolery has lost its force,
Aye, stiffens up, as 'twere a puppet king,
If but a menial murmurs "Majesty";
The habit of a lifetime holding good
To gratify the Hohenzollern pride.
Second Guard—The people murmur many
      other things
And loudly too, which though far off, remote,
Yet echo here.   From Prussia, Austria;—
The German border is a dyke that leaks
And every courier—
First Guard—   Yea, he starts in fear
And trembles, shrinks, if one but lifts the
      hand,
Or takes a sudden step, or raises voice,
Or stirs the wind among the shrubbery,
Or there is deep commotion at the gate.
Ah, 'tis to laugh indeed.   Caesar is nought;
A nothing; but lives on.—
Second Guard—   Lives on, you say;
Had he been Roman he had used the sword

Like Nero cried "See how an artist dies!"
But being lesser clay he lives, and so
The comedy is finished!
First Guard—   And begun
The Tragedy!   (*The door of the house opens
    abruptly*)
Second Guard—(*stepping aside and toward
    the house*)
                    No, after you; he comes;
Hist, silence!
*They stand attention as a heavily muffled
figure totters out for the evening walk with a
companion and as it salutes the guards they
return the courtesy with a scarcely whispered
and hardly disguised ironical*
          Zu Befehl, Ihr Majestät!
*As it disappears in the grounds they go within
while in .the distance is heard the menacing
melancholy wail of the Belgian refugees
trudging homeward along the public highway:*
"Guillaume, Assassin! Assassin, Guillaume!!"

Und der Vorhang fällt schnell und immerfort.

CPSIA information can be obtained
at www.ICGtesting.com
Printed in the USA
BVOW03*2148130917
494820BV00004B/10/P